sandwiches!

sandwiches!

grilled • toasted • bruschetta • ciabatta • focaccia

This edition published in 2010
LOVE FOOD is an imprint of Parragon Books Ltd

Parragon
Queen Street House
4 Queen Street
Bath BA1 1HE, UK

ISBN 978-1-4454-1075-3

Printed in China

Internal design by Talking Design
Photography by Bob Wheeler
Home economy by Valerie Barrett and Sandra Baddeley
Additional recipes and text by Bridget Jones

NOTES FOR THE READER

This book uses imperial, metric, and U.S. cup measurements. Follow the same units of
measurement throughout, do not mix imperial and metric.

All spoon measurements are level: teaspoons are assumed to be 5 ml, and tablespoons are
assumed to be 15 ml.

Unless otherwise stated, milk is assumed to be whole, eggs and individual vegetables such as
potatoes are medium, and pepper is freshly ground black pepper. The times given are an
approximate guide only.

Some recipes contain nuts. If you are allergic to nuts you should avoid using them and any
products containing nuts. Recipes using raw or very lightly cooked eggs should be avoided by
infants, the elderly, pregnant women, convalescents, and anyone with a chronic condition.

Contents

Introduction

Toasting to perfection—the right thickness, temperature, and texture—is easy with a little attention to ingredients and technique. Adding toppings or fillings, experimenting with different breads, and toasting for all occasions is about fun cooking and fabulous eating!

Breads

Country style, fine, close-textured bread toasts evenly and becomes crisp outside and soft inside without collapsing or becoming sticky inside when hot. Toasted slowly, thinly sliced bread becomes very crisp.

Whole wheat, rye, and mixed-grain breads make delicious, nutty toast, and walnut and seeded breads are good for topping or filling. Semi-sweet fruit breads are excellent buttered, with sweet spreads, or topped with fruit and broiled.

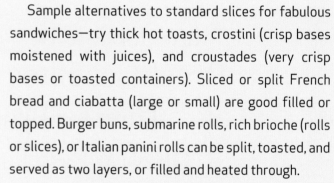

Sample alternatives to standard slices for fabulous sandwiches—try thick hot toasts, crostini (crisp bases moistened with juices), and croustades (very crisp bases or toasted containers). Sliced or split French bread and ciabatta (large or small) are good filled or topped. Burger buns, submarine rolls, rich brioche (rolls or slices), or Italian panini rolls can be split, toasted, and served as two layers, or filled and heated through.

Try croissants or waffles for different shapes and textures. Top focaccia, flatbreads, Indian naan, or Greek pitta; toast tortilla wraps, plain or filled.

Spreads and Fats

Good butter is the only topper for plain toast—lightly salted, or salted, but not sweet dairy. Low-fat spreads, and reduced-fat butters make toast soggy. Olive oil is delicious for savory toasts—brush it lightly on the top side of the bread before broiling. Smooth or crunchy peanut butter is good—make sure it is at room temperature, not chilled. There's no need for fat under toasted cheese as fat forms a barrier under moist toppings that quickly make toast soft.

Equipment

• **Broiler** Versatile for broiling all sorts of breads, toppings, and fillings, or heating layers. Vary temperature settings and distance from the heat source to control cooking. Place food on a rack in a broiler pan for fat to drip away and to keep the underside crisp; cook on foil to catch juices or toppings that run.

• **Griddle** A ridged griddle can be used on the hob or (with suitable handles) under the broiler. On the hob, this gives characteristic stripes at high heat, or the food gradually grills evenly if the griddle is not fiercely hot. Under the broiler, a griddle will cook the underside as the top toasts.

• **Sandwich toaster or tabletop grill** Two hot plates that cook sandwiches easily. Light fillings, which cook quickly from raw, go on the hottest setting; reduce the heat for heavier fillings. Some are indented for making deep-filled sandwiches, or have griddle plates that rest slightly apart for cooking toppings.

• **Pop-up toaster** Variable settings are essential for evenly toasting breads of different thickness, or from frozen. Many take different types of bread such as waffles or croissants. Special nonstick cooking bags can be used for sandwiches.

• **Toasting fork** Traditional for grills or log fires. Large or small expanding forks are great for marshmallows or chunks of bread.

Breakfast
Bites

Perfect Toast

makes 1 slice

Preheat the broiler on a medium–high setting and warm a plate (putting hot toast on a cold plate produces condensation, making the underneath of the toast soggy). Place the bread on a rack in the broiler pan and toast for about 2 minutes on each side, until evenly golden and crisp. Turn once.

Take the pan from under the broiler but leave the toast on the rack. Have the butter ready and spread it on top of the freshly toasted surface. Immediately transfer the toast to the warmed plate, cut it in half with a serrated knife and enjoy plain or with a topping of your choice.

ingredients

1 slice traditional white bread, or bread of your choice, $3/4$ inches/ 1.5 cm thick

about 1 tbsp butter, softened

topping of your choice, such as chocolate spread or raspberry jelly

Hot Smoked Salmon, Tomato &
Cream Cheese Bagel

serves 2

Preheat the broiler on a medium–high setting. Slice the bagels in half horizontally and place them cut sides down on the rack in the broiler pan. Toast until browned, then turn over.

Cover the bottom halves of the bagels with tomato slices. Sprinkle with lemon zest and scallion, then season with pepper (but not salt—the smoked salmon will be salty when cooked). Trickle a hint of olive oil over the tomatoes. Broil for 1–2 minutes, until the bagels are toasted and the tomatoes are lightly cooked. Remove the top halves and set aside.

Arrange the smoked salmon slices on the tomatoes, wrinkling them slightly, and replace them under the broiler for a minute, to lightly cook the salmon and brown the edges in places.

Top each with a couple of dollops of cream cheese and the bagel lids. Serve at once, with lemon wedges, for adding a squeeze of juice.

ingredients

2 bagels

2 tomatoes, thinly sliced

grated zest of 1 lemon

1 scallion, chopped

pepper

olive oil

4 slices smoked salmon (about $4^{1}/_{2}$ oz/130 g)

4 tbsp cream cheese

lemon wedges, to serve

Toasted Cheese & Ham Sandwich with Egg

serves 1

Preheat the broiler on a medium–high setting. Prepare a small pan of simmering water or an egg poacher. Warm a serving plate.

Top a slice of bread with ham. Trim off any large areas of overlapping ham and place them on top. Overlap the tomato slices on the ham and sprinkle with the snipped chives and parsley sprigs. Top with the cheese slices. Season with pepper (there will probably be enough salt in the ham) and drizzle with a little olive oil, then cover with the second slice of bread.

Toast the sandwich on both sides until crisp and golden. Meanwhile, break the egg into a cup. Swirl the simmering water and drop the egg into the middle of the swirl, then poach it for about 3 minutes, until the white is set and the yolk still soft. (Cook the egg for a shorter or longer time, to taste.) Alternatively, cook the egg in a poaching pan with cups. Use a slotted spoon to lift the egg from the pan, draining it thoroughly.

Serve the sandwich on a warmed plate, topped with the poached egg. Top with a little butter, if liked, so that it melts over the egg. Serve immediately.

ingredients

2 slices good white or whole wheat bread

1 thick slice cooked ham

1 large tomato, thinly sliced

about 1 tbsp snipped fresh chives

small bunch of fresh flat-leaf parsley, stalks discarded

2 slices mild cheese, such as Monterey or mild cheddar

pepper

olive oil

1 egg

a little soft butter (optional)

Toasted English Muffins with Blueberries & Bacon

serves 2

Preheat the broiler on a medium–high setting. Slice the muffins in half horizontally and place them, cut sides down, on the rack in the broiler pan.

Lay the bacon on the rack and cook until the tops of the muffins are toasted and the bacon is lightly cooked on one side.

Turn the muffins and divide the blueberries among the bottom halves. Invert the bacon on to the blueberries, covering them completely. Cook for a further 2 minutes, removing the top halves as soon as they are toasted and the bottom halves when the bacon is browned and crisp.

Place the muffin bases on warmed plates, drizzle with maple syrup or honey, and add the muffin tops. Serve at once.

ingredients

2 English muffins

4 lean bacon slices

1 cup blueberries

2 tsp maple syrup or clear honey

Ham & Cheese Croissant

serves 1

Preheat the broiler on a medium–high setting. Slice the croissant horizontally in half, then lay it, cut sides up, on a piece of cooking foil on the rack in the broiler pan.

Top each croissant with two half slices of cooked ham, overlapping the halves, and spread with a little mustard, if liked. Then top with the cheese, cutting and overlapping the slices to fit the croissant. Broil for about 2 minutes, until the cheese has melted. The croissant will be warmed through and beginning to brown around the edges.

If including the egg, overlap the slices on the bottom half of the croissant. Use a knife to scoop any melted cheese off the foil and onto the croissant, then invert the top in place. Serve at once.

ingredients

1 croissant

2 thin slices cooked ham, halved

mustard (optional)

2 slices hard cheese, such as Cheddar, Gruyère, or Emmental (about 1 oz/25 g)

1 egg, hard-cooked and sliced (optional)

French Toast
with Maple Syrup

serves 4–6

Preheat the oven to 275°F/140°C. Break the eggs into a large, shallow bowl and beat together with the milk, cinnamon, and salt to taste. Add the bread slices and press them down so that they are covered on both sides with the egg mixture. Leave the bread to stand for 1–2 minutes to soak up the egg mixture, turning the slices over once.

Melt half the butter with 1/2 tablespoon of oil in a large skillet. Add as many bread slices to the pan as will fit in a single layer and cook for 2–3 minutes until golden brown.

Turn the bread slices over and cook until golden brown on the other side. Transfer the French toast to a plate and keep warm in the oven while cooking the remaining bread slices, adding extra oil if necessary.

Serve the French toast with the remaining butter melting on top and warm maple syrup for pouring over.

ingredients

6 eggs

3/4 cup milk

1/4 tsp ground cinnamon

salt

12 slices day-old challah or plain white bread

about 4 tbsp butter or margarine, plus extra to serve

1/2 –1 tbsp sunflower-seed or corn oil

warm maple syrup, to serve

Toasted English Muffins with Honey-glazed Bacon & Eggs

serves 2

Preheat the broiler on a medium–high setting. Slice the muffins horizontally in half, then lay them cut sides up on a piece of cooking foil on the rack in the broiler pan. Toast until lightly browned, then turn and cook on the other side. Reserve and keep warm.

Preheat the oven to 275°F/140°C. Heat a nonstick skillet over medium heat. Lay the bacon slices in the skillet and cook until lightly browned, then turn and cook the other side.

Warm the honey slightly and brush each bacon slice lightly with it. Cook the bacon for an additional 1 minute or until it takes on a slight glaze. Remove from the pan and keep warm in the preheated oven.

Mix the corn, diced tomatoes, and chopped parsley together in a bowl and season to taste with salt and pepper. Fry, poach, or scramble the eggs, as you prefer.

Serve the honey-glazed bacon and eggs on the toasted muffins, on warmed plates. Top each with a spoonful of the corn and tomato mixture.

ingredients

2 English muffins

6 rindless unsmoked bacon slices

1 tbsp honey

3 oz/85 g canned corn kernels, drained

2 small tomatoes, diced

1 tbsp chopped fresh parsley

salt and pepper

4 eggs

butter

Croque Monsieur

serves 2

Spread the cheese on 2 slices of bread and top each with a slice of ham and the remaining bread.

For the sauce, melt the butter with the oil in a small, heavy-bottom pan and stir in the flour until well combined and smooth. Remove from the heat and stir in a little of the milk until well incorporated. Return to the heat and gradually add the remaining milk, stirring constantly, until it has all been incorporated. Cook for an additional 3 minutes, or until the sauce is smooth and thickened. Remove the pan from the heat and stir in the cheese and pepper. Set aside and keep warm.

Beat the egg in a bowl. Add 1 sandwich and press down to coat on both sides, then remove from the dish and repeat with the other sandwich. Preheat the broiler to high. Melt the butter in a skillet over a medium–high heat and fry the sandwiches until golden brown on both sides.

Transfer the sandwiches to a cookie sheet and spread the white sauce over the top. Cook under the broiler, about 4 inches/10 cm from the heat, for 4 minutes, or until golden and brown.

ingredients

2 oz/50 g Gruyère or Emmental cheese, grated

4 slices white bread, with the crusts trimmed

2 thick slices ham

1 small egg, beaten

3 tbsp unsalted butter, plus extra if necessary

for the cheese sauce

2 tbsp unsalted butter

1 tsp corn oil

$1/2$ tbsp all-purpose flour

$1/2$ cup warmed milk

2 oz/50 g Gruyère or Emmental cheese, grated

pepper

Chive Scrambled
Eggs with Brioche

serves 2

Break the eggs into a medium-sized bowl and whisk gently with the cream. Season to taste with salt and pepper and add the snipped chives.

Melt the butter in a sauté pan and pour in the egg mixture. Let set slightly, then move the mixture toward the center of the pan using a wooden spoon as the eggs start to cook. Continue in this way until the eggs are cooked but still creamy.

Lightly toast the brioche slices in a toaster or under the broiler and place in the center of two warmed plates. Spoon over the scrambled eggs and serve immediately, garnished with the whole chives.

ingredients

4 eggs

$1/3$ cup light cream

salt and pepper

2 tbsp snipped fresh chives, plus 4 whole fresh chives for garnishing

2 tbsp butter

4 slices brioche loaf

Time for Brunch

Minted Summer
Brie on Pita

serves 2

Cut the brie into two equal wedges, then slice them horizontally into two layers and replace in the freezer to keep the cheese very firm, but not frozen. Reserve a couple of mint sprigs for garnish, then discard the stalks from the others and shred the leaves.

Preheat the broiler on a medium–high setting. Toast the pita breads on one side, then place them, untoasted sides up, onto a piece of cooking foil on the rack in the broiler pan.

Cover the pita with the cucumber, taking the slices right over the edge, and sprinkle with the mint. Season lightly with salt and pepper. Use a pair of scissors to snip the sundried tomatoes into thin strips, sprinkling them evenly over the breads. Top with the brie, laying the wedges cut sides down, with the rind up.

Drizzle a little oil over the brie and place under the broiler for 2–4 minutes, until the rind is browned, and the cheese runny. Stir the Greek-style yogurt and spoon a little on the breads. Garnish with the reserved mint sprigs and serve immediately.

ingredients

6 oz/170 g wedge of brie, chilled in the freezer

6 fresh mint sprigs

2 pita breads

$1/4$ cucumber (about 4 inches/ 10 cm), thinly sliced

salt and pepper

10 sundried tomatoes in oil, drained (about 2 oz/55 g)

olive oil

2 tbsp Greek-style yogurt

Salami, Bell Pepper & Pine Nut Panini

serves 2

Preheat the broiler on a medium–high setting. Lay a piece of cooking foil on the rack in the broiler pan. Mix the pepper strips and garlic in a heap on the foil. Drizzle with a little olive oil, turn the strips to coat them lightly, and then spread them out.

Lay the bread halves cut sides down on the foil around the pepper strips. Cook for about 1 minute to lightly toast the breads, then remove them, and continue cooking the pepper strips for 2–3 minutes or until they begin to brown.

Replace the bread on the foil, cut sides up. Cover the bottom layers of bread with the salami and basil leaves. Add the pepper strips and sprinkle with the pine nuts. Cut the radicchio into wedges and arrange them on top. Drizzle with a little oil, and broil for 2–3 minutes, until beginning to wilt and brown at the edges. Remove the top layers of bread as soon as they are toasted.

Sprinkle with Parmesan or pecorino, add the bread tops, and serve immediately.

ingredients

1 large red bell pepper, seeded and cut into thin strips

2 garlic cloves, sliced

olive oil

2 panini rolls or individual ciabatta, split horizontally

6 salami slices

handful of fresh basil leaves

1 tbsp pine nuts

1 small head of radicchio or endive, quartered

Parmesan or pecorino shavings

Mozzarella-broiled Panini with Chile-Spiked Shrimp & Olives

serves 2

Preheat the broiler on a medium–high setting. Dry the shrimp on paper towels and place them in a bowl. Add the chile, scallions, olives, and garlic, if liked. Stir in the lemon zest and juice, parsley, and seasoning to taste.

Slice the bread horizontally in two and place the bottom halves, cut sides down, on a piece of cooking foil on the rack in the broiler pan. Lay the top halves on the foil, cut sides up. Toast the breads for 1–2 minutes until browned and crisp.

Turn the breads over. Divide the shrimp mixture among the bottom halves, piling it in place and making sure the breads are covered. Arrange the mozzarella slices on the top halves. Drizzle a hint of olive oil over the shrimp mixture and on the mozzarella, but take care not to add too much or the bread will be greasy.

Place under the broiler until the shrimp filling is hot and the mozzarella is melted and bubbling. Use a palette knife to lift the panini lids on top of the shrimp filling, scraping up any mozzarella that may have drizzled off the bread. Serve immediately.

ingredients

2 cups peeled cooked shrimp, thawed if frozen

1 fresh green chile, seeded and chopped

2 scallions, chopped

$1/2$ cup pitted black olives, halved

1 garlic clove, chopped (optional)

grated zest of 1 lemon and squeeze of lemon juice

2 panini rolls or individual ciabatta

small handful of parsley, trimmed and roughly chopped

salt and pepper

1 ball mozzarella cheese (about 5 oz/140 g), thinly sliced

olive oil

Chorizo & Fennel Crostini

serves 4–6

Preheat the broiler on a medium–high setting. Cover the rack in the broiler pan with a piece of cooking foil. Place the slices of bread on the foil and brush with olive oil. Toast for about 3 minutes, until crisp and golden.

Meanwhile, shred the fennel finely. Mix the fennel and onion with seasoning and a little olive oil in a bowl, adding just enough oil to moisten the vegetables. Separate the onion into curvy strips as you mix. Cut the top and bottom off the grapefruit, then cut off all the rind and pith working down around the sides. Cut out the segments from between the membranes. Turn the bread over, brush with olive oil and cover with the fennel mixture. Broil for a further 3 minutes, until the vegetables are lightly cooked and beginning to brown. Increase the heat to the hottest setting. Top the crostini with grapefruit segments, and then cover with slices of chorizo. Brush or drizzle with a little olive oil and broil for about 1 minute, until the chorizo is sizzling, curling a little, and beginning to brown.

Top with crème fraîche, sprinkle with chopped fresh cilantro, and serve immediately.

ingredients

12 slices French bread (about 1 inch/2.5 cm thick)

olive oil

1 fennel bulb

1 red onion, halved and thinly sliced

salt and pepper

1 pink grapefruit

24 thin slices chorizo (about 4$1/2$ oz/130 g)

4 tbsp crème fraîche

2 tbsp chopped fresh cilantro leaves

Sausage &
Mushroom Brioche

serves 2–4

Use a vegetable peeler to pare the carrots into fine strips. Place in a bowl of cold water, then add ice and set aside for about 30 minutes.

Preheat the broiler on a medium–high setting. Broil the sausages for about 15 minutes, turning once or twice, until browned and almost cooked.

In a bowl, mix together the tarragon, garlic, oil, and orange rind and juice. Mix half the dressing with the mushrooms then toast the brioche lightly on both sides in a toaster.

Increase the heat to the hottest setting. Place the brioche on the rack in the broiler pan. Cover with mushrooms up to the edges of the bread (otherwise it will burn). Broil close to the heat source for 2–4 minutes until lightly cooked.

Slice the sausages and arrange them on the mushrooms. Broil well away from the heat for about 5 minutes, until the sausages are browned.

Drain the carrots. Arrange the corn salad or other salad leaves on plates and drizzle with the remaining dressing. Add the toasts and top with the carrot curls. Serve immediately.

ingredients

2 large carrots

4 fresh chunky Italian sausages (about 1 lb/450 g)

6 fresh tarragon sprigs, leaves only

1 garlic clove, chopped

4 tbsp olive oil

grated zest and juice of 1 orange

7 oz/200 g open chestnut mushrooms or shiitake, thickly sliced

4 thick slices good brioche loaf (plain, not sweetened or flavored with vanilla)

corn salad or other salad leaves, to serve

Brunch
Bruschetta

serves 2

Preheat the broiler on a medium–high setting. Lay the ciabatta on a piece of cooking foil on the rack in the broiler pan. Toast until lightly browned, then turn and cook on the other side. Reserve and keep warm.

Mix the tomato, scallions, cheese, avocado, balsamic vinegar, and half of the oil together in a medium bowl. Season to taste with salt and pepper.

Drizzle the remaining oil over the ciabatta toast and top with the tomato mixture. Garnish with basil and serve at once.

ingredients

4 slices ciabatta bread

1 large ripe tomato, diced

2 scallions, finely sliced

1 small fresh buffalo mozzarella cheese, diced

$1/2$ ripe avocado, diced

$1/2$ tbsp balsamic vinegar

2 tbsp extra virgin olive oil

salt and pepper

2 tbsp shredded fresh basil leaves, to garnish

Basque
Scrambled Eggs

serves 4–6

Preheat the broiler on a medium–high setting. Lay the bread on a piece of cooking foil on the rack in the broiler pan. Toast until lightly browned, then turn and cook on the other side. Keep warm.

Heat 2 tablespoons of oil in a large, heavy-bottom skillet over medium–high heat. Add the onion and bell peppers and cook for about 5 minutes, or until the vegetables are soft, but not brown. Add the tomatoes and heat through. Transfer to a plate and keep warm in a preheated low oven.

Add another tablespoon of oil to the skillet. Add the chorizo and cook for 30 seconds, just to warm through and flavor the oil. Add the sausage to the reserved vegetables.

There should be about 2 tablespoons of oil in the skillet, so add a little extra, if necessary, to make up the amount. Add the butter and let melt. Season the eggs with salt and pepper, then add them to the skillet. Scramble the eggs until they are cooked to the desired degree of firmness. Add extra seasoning to taste. Return the vegetables to the skillet and stir through. Serve at once with the hot toast.

ingredients

4–6 thick slices country-style bread

olive oil

1 large onion, chopped finely

1 large red bell pepper, cored, seeded, and chopped

1 large green bell pepper, cored, seeded, and chopped

2 large tomatoes, peeled, seeded, and chopped

2 oz/55 g chorizo sausage, sliced thinly, casings removed, if preferred

3 tbsp butter

10 large eggs, beaten lightly

salt and pepper

Bagels with Leeks & Cheese

serves 2

Preheat the broiler on a medium–high setting. Lay the bagels bottom side up on a piece of cooking foil. Toast until lightly browned, repeat on the other side, then reserve and keep warm.

Trim the leeks, discarding the green ends, and split down the center, leaving the root intact. Wash well to remove any grit and slice finely, discarding the root.

Melt the butter over low heat in a large sauté pan and add the leeks. Cook, stirring constantly, for 5 minutes, or until the leeks are soft and slightly browned. Let cool.

Preheat the broiler. Mix the cooled leeks, grated cheese, scallions, parsley, and salt and pepper to taste together. Spread the cheese mixture over the top of each bagel and place under the preheated broiler until bubbling and golden brown. Serve at once.

ingredients

2 fresh bagels

2 leeks

2 tbsp butter

1 cup grated Gruyère cheese

2 scallions, finely chopped

1 tbsp chopped fresh parsley

salt and pepper

Cheese & Sun-dried
Tomato Toasts

serves 4

Preheat the broiler on a medium–high setting and preheat the oven to 425°F/220°C. Slice the loaves diagonally and discard the end pieces. Toast the slices on both sides under the broiler until golden.

Spread one side of each toast with the sun-dried tomato paste and top with mozzarella. Sprinkle with oregano and season to taste with pepper.

Put the toasts on a large baking sheet and drizzle with oil. Bake in the preheated oven for 5 minutes, or until the cheese is melted and bubbling. Remove the toasts from the oven and let stand for 5 minutes before serving.

ingredients

2 small French loaves

$3/4$ cup sun-dried tomato paste

1 small ball fresh buffalo mozzarella

$1^1/_2$ tsp dried oregano

pepper

2–3 tbsp olive oil

Mushroom
Bruschetta

serves 4

Preheat the broiler on a medium–high setting. Toast the bread under the broiler until golden on both sides. Reserve and keep warm.

Meanwhile, heat the oil in a skillet. Add the garlic and cook gently for a few seconds, then add the cremini mushrooms. Cook, stirring constantly, over high heat for 3 minutes. Add the wild mushrooms and cook for an additional 2 minutes. Stir in the lemon juice.

Season to taste with salt and pepper and stir in the chopped parsley.

Spoon the mushroom mixture onto the warm toast and serve.

ingredients

12 slices French baguette, each $1/2$ inch/1 cm thick, or 2 individual French baguettes, cut lengthwise

3 tbsp olive oil

2 garlic cloves, crushed

8 oz/225 g cremini mushrooms, sliced

8 oz/225 g mixed wild mushrooms

2 tsp lemon juice

salt and pepper

2 tbsp chopped fresh parsley

Spicy Broiled
Feta Cheese on Ciabatta Toast

serves 2

Preheat the broiler on a medium–high setting. Toast either side of the ciabatta slices until golden brown. Place the toasted ciabatta slices on a baking sheet and cover each with a generous slice of feta cheese. Mix the oil, red chile flakes, and oregano together and drizzle evenly over the cheese.

Broil for 2–3 minutes, or until the cheese starts to melt, and place on serving plates. Drizzle over a little extra oil and serve with arugula leaves.

ingredients

4 slices ciabatta bread

7 oz/200 g feta cheese

2 tbsp olive oil, plus extra for drizzling

1 tsp dried red chile flakes

1 tsp dried oregano

scant 2 cups arugula leaves, to serve

Quick & Easy
Lunches

Perfect Broiled Cheese Sandwich

serves 4

Slice the crusty top off the loaf; reserve for another use. Slice the loaf into two, horizontally, making the bottom thicker. Place the bottom on a large piece of cooking foil.

Preheat the broiler on a medium–high setting. Toast the top surface of the top layer of the loaf until brown, then turn it and place on the foil.

Sprinkle some cheese over both layers of bread. Arrange avocado slices and tomato wedges on the bottom layer then sprinkle with half the remaining cheese. Top with the asparagus spears and ham, completely covering the edges of the ingredients underneath. Sprinkle with the remaining cheese, pepper to taste, and a trickle of olive oil.

Cook well away from the heat source for 3–5 minutes. Remove the plain cheese-topped layer first, when the cheese is bubbling. Cook the bottom layer until the cheese has melted and the ham is browned.

Cut the toasted cheese layer into 8 wedges and overlap them on the filling, alternating the plain and cheese sides up. Serve at once, cut into four wedges.

ingredients

1 stoneground buckwheat boule loaf (about 7 inches/17.5 cm in diameter) or other rustic round loaf

6 oz/170 g Cheddar cheese, finely shaved or coarsely shredded

1 large avocado, halved, pitted, peeled, and sliced

2 tomatoes, halved and cut into fine wedges

12 asparagus spears, cooked, bottled or canned

4 slices Parma, Serrano or Black Forest ham

pepper

olive oil

Smoked Chicken & Ham Focaccia

serves 2–4

Preheat a griddle plate or pan under the broiler until both broiler and griddle are hot. If you do not have a griddle, heat a heavy baking sheet or roasting pan instead. Slice the thick focaccia in half horizontally and cut the top half into strips. If using slightly thinner flatbread, leave one whole and slice the second bread into strips.

Cover the bottom half of the focaccia (or whole bread) with basil leaves, top with the zucchini in an even layer, and then cover with the chicken and ham, alternating the slices, and wrinkling them. Lay the strips of focaccia on top, placing strips of Taleggio cheese between them. Sprinkle with a little nutmeg if liked.

Place the assembled bread on the hot griddle and cook under the broiler, well away from the heat, for about 5 minutes, until the Taleggio has melted, and the top of the bread is browned. Serve immediately with cherry tomatoes if liked.

ingredients

1 thick focaccia loaf (about 6–7 inches/15–17 cm) or 2 Italian flatbreads

handful of basil leaves

2 small zucchini, coarsely shredded

6 paper-thin slices of smoked chicken

6 paper-thin slices of cooked ham

8 oz/225 g Taleggio cheese, cut into strips

freshly grated nutmeg (optional)

cherry tomatoes, to serve (optional)

Roasted Bell Pepper Ciabatta with Chopped Eggs & Olives

serves 2–4

Place the eggs in a small pan, add hot water to cover and bring to a boil. Reduce the heat and simmer for 8 minutes. Drain, rinse under cold water, and peel the eggs, then chop them, and place in a bowl. Add the olives and cilantro, with seasoning to taste, fork the ingredients together, and set aside.

Preheat the broiler on a medium–high setting. Mix the red, green, and yellow pepper strips with the onion, garlic, oregano, and olive oil. Season to taste.

Slice the ciabatta in half horizontally. Place cut sides down on the rack in a broiler pan and toast the tops for about a minute, until crisp and lightly browned. Turn the bread. Arrange the pepper strips on the bread, covering it completely. Sprinkle the onion, garlic, and oregano over as you go, and drizzle any remaining oil over.

Toast the pepper-topped breads for 4–5 minutes, until the peppers are softened and well browned in places. Top with the egg mixture, and add lemon wedges so that their juice can be sprinkled over. Serve immediately.

ingredients

2 eggs

1/2 cup pitted black olives, chopped

2 tbsp chopped fresh cilantro leaves

1 large red bell pepper, seeded and cut into thin strips

1 large green bell pepper, seeded and cut into thin strips

1 large yellow bell pepper, seeded and cut into thin strips

1 small red onion, finely chopped

1 garlic clove, finely chopped

1 tbsp chopped fresh oregano

2 tbsp olive oil

salt and pepper

1 large ciabatta loaf

lemon wedges, to serve

Tempting Tomato
Bruschetta

serves 4

Mix the tomato paste, mustard, garlic, sugar, and vinegar in a bowl large enough to hold all the other ingredients. Whisk in 2 tbsp of the oil until thoroughly combined.

Preheat the broiler on a medium–high setting. Place the slices of bread on the rack in the broiler pan, and brush lightly with oil, then toast until crisp and golden.

Meanwhile, add the scallions, thyme, and parsley to the tomato mixture, and mix thoroughly. Stir in the diced tomatoes until they are thoroughly combined with the other ingredients. Add seasoning to taste.

Turn the bread slices and cover the untoasted sides with the tomato mixture, using a teaspoon to nudge the tomatoes and their juices right up to the edges. Slide the bruschetta close together and cook under the broiler, not too close to the heat, for 4–5 minutes, until lightly browned in places.

Transfer to a platter, garnish with herb sprigs, and drizzle with a hint of olive oil. Serve at once.

ingredients

2 tbsp tomato paste

1 tbsp mustard, such as Dijon or wholegrain

2 garlic cloves, crushed

$1/2$ tsp sugar

1 tbsp apple cider vinegar

about 4 tbsp extra virgin olive oil, plus extra for serving

12 slices good French bread

4 scallions, chopped

2 tbsp fresh thyme leaves

handful of chopped parsley, stalks discarded

6 tomatoes, diced

salt and pepper

herb sprigs, to garnish

Salad Greek Crostini

serves 2

Preheat the broiler on a medium–high setting. Mix the garlic and olive oil in a bowl large enough to hold all the salad ingredients.

Place the bread on the rack in the broiler pan. Brush lightly with the garlic oil and toast well away from the heat for 2–3 minutes, until crisp and golden. Turn the bread and cover with the halloumi cheese, taking it right up to the crusty edges. Brush with more garlic oil, then toast again for 3–4 minutes, until the halloumi is browned, crisp on top, and tender under its crust.

Meanwhile, add the cucumber, olives, tomatoes, onion, mint, oregano, and sugar to the oil remaining in the bowl, and mix well. Lightly mix in the lettuce. Divide the salad among two plates and sprinkle with sesame seeds.

Transfer the hot crostini to the plates, add the salad, and serve immediately.

ingredients

1 garlic clove, crushed

4 tbsp olive oil

2 thick slices of a large sesame seed bloomer

9 oz/250 g halloumi cheese, sliced

pepper

$1/4$ cucumber, finely diced

$1/4$ cup black olives, thinly sliced

2 large ripe plum tomatoes, diced

$1/2$ small mild onion, finely chopped

2 sprigs fresh mint leaves, shredded

2 sprigs fresh oregano leaves, chopped

pinch of sugar

1 heart Bibb lettuce, finely shredded

1 tsp toasted sesame seeds

Sherried Chicken & Bacon Toasts

serves 2

Heat the oil in a skillet and add the bacon, onion, garlic, bay leaf, and thyme. Cook, stirring often, for 5 minutes, until the bacon and onion are cooked. Add the chicken, and continue cooking for 5 minutes, stirring so that the chicken cooks evenly.

Add the mustard and sherry and bring to a boil, stirring all the sediment off the bottom of the pan. Add seasoning to taste. Simmer for 3–4 minutes, until the sherry is reduced to a mustard-glaze on the ingredients. Discard the bay leaf and herb sprigs.

Meanwhile, preheat the broiler on a medium–high setting and warm two plates. Place the bread on a rack in the broiler pan, and toast for about 2 minutes on each side, until evenly golden and crisp.

Butter the hot toast and place on the plates. Stir the parsley into the chicken mixture and pile it on the toasts. Drizzle over a little yogurt, if liked, then serve immediately.

ingredients

2 tbsp olive oil

2 rindless bacon slices, cut into strips

1 small onion, chopped

2 garlic cloves, chopped

1 bay leaf

2 fresh thyme sprigs

2 small boneless skinless chicken breasts, cut into small chunks

1 tbsp whole grain mustard

6 tbsp dry sherry

salt and pepper

2 slices traditional white bread, $3/4$ inch/1.5 cm thick

about 1 tbsp butter, softened

small handful of chopped parsley, stalks discarded

2 tbsp mild plain yogurt (optional)

Rye Toast with
Roast Beef & Coleslaw

serves 1–2

Preheat a sandwich toaster, the broiler, or a griddle. Mix the ginger with the butter.

Spread one slice of bread generously with some of the butter. Top with the cabbage, trimming any overhanging shreds and placing them back on the middle of the sandwich. Top with carrot and scallion, keeping them away from the edge. Season lightly.

Spread a little more of the butter on one side of the beef and lay it, butter down, on the carrot. Spread the remaining butter on the second slice of bread and place it on top of the sandwich, buttered side down.

Toast the sandwich in the toaster, under the broiler (well away from the heat), or on a griddle, until crisp and golden. Turn it over once when cooking under the broiler or on the griddle, to cook both sides. Serve at once, with dill pickles, if liked.

ingredients

1 tbsp finely chopped fresh gingerroot or horseradish sauce

$1^1/_2$ tbsp butter, softened

2 slices light rye bread, preferably with caraway seeds

1 very thinly sliced cabbage (white or firm green heart)

1 small carrot, coarsely shredded

1 scallion, sliced

salt and pepper

1 large slice roast beef

dill pickles, to serve (optional)

Turkey
Ciabatta with Walnuts

serves 2

Preheat the broiler on a medium–high setting. Slice the ciabatta rolls in half horizontally and toast the cut sides under the grill. Remove the top halves. Turn the bottom halves and toast the undersides until brown and crisp. When the breads are toasted, reduce the heat to a low setting.

Meanwhile, mix the blue cheese, walnuts, and sage. Lay the turkey slices on the bases of the rolls and top with the cheese and walnut mixture, piling it up in the middle. Cover with the tops of the rolls.

Heat the rolls under the broiler, well away from the heat, for 3–4 minutes, until the breads are hot, and the cheese is beginning to melt. Increase the heat slightly, if necessary, to a medium setting, but do not turn it up high enough to brown the tops of the rolls before they are warmed through.

Serve the hot rolls with green grapes as an accompaniment.

ingredients

2 ciabatta rolls

4 oz/115 g blue cheese, such as Stilton or Danish blue, finely diced or crumbled

$3/4$ cup walnuts, chopped

8 large fresh sage leaves, finely shredded

4 slices cooked turkey breast

seedless green grapes, to serve

Crab Cake Toasts

serves 2–4

Place one piece of bread on a plate and spoon the milk evenly over it. Let stand for a few minutes. Brush the remaining slices lightly on both sides with butter.

Mix the crabmeat, chile, and scallion in a bowl. Mash the soaked bread with a fork and mix it with the crabmeat, scraping in the milk off the plate. Stir in the remaining melted butter and season to taste.

Preheat the broiler on a medium–high setting and toast the buttered bread until crisp and golden on both sides. Top with the crab mixture, spreading it evenly right over the edges, and forking the surface slightly so that it is not too smooth.

Place under the broiler for about 3 minutes, until the creamy topping is browned. Serve at once, garnished with lemon wedges so that their juice can be squeezed over the crab.

ingredients

3 slices good white bread, crusts removed

2 tbsp milk

2 tbsp butter, melted

6 oz/170 g canned crabmeat, drained, or 5 oz/140 g fresh or frozen crabmeat, thawed if frozen

1 green chile, seeded and chopped

1 scallion, finely chopped

salt and pepper

lemon wedges, to garnish

Tuscan Beans on Ciabatta Toast with Fresh Herbs

serves 2

Preheat the broiler on a medium–high setting. Place the bread on a rack in the broiler pan and toast until lightly browned, then turn and cook on the other side. Reserve and keep warm.

Heat the oil in a medium sauté pan and cook the onion over low heat until soft. Add the garlic and cook for an additional 1 minute, then add the lima beans, water, and tomato paste. Bring to a boil, stirring occasionally, and cook for 2 minutes.

Add the balsamic vinegar, parsley, and basil and stir to combine. Season to taste with salt and pepper and serve over slices of the toasted ciabatta.

ingredients

2 slices ciabatta

1 tbsp olive oil

1 small onion, finely diced

1 garlic clove, crushed

9 oz/250 g canned lima beans, drained and rinsed

$1/3$ cup water

1 tbsp tomato paste

1 tsp balsamic vinegar

1 tbsp chopped fresh parsley

1 tbsp torn fresh basil

salt and pepper

Something Special

Salmon & Watercress Ciabatta

serves 2

Preheat the broiler on a medium–high setting. Slice the ciabbata in half horizontally and place cut sides down on the rack in the broiler pan. Toast until browned.

Cut the salmon fillet into $1/2$-inch/1-cm-thick slices and place in a large shallow flameproof dish. Sprinkle the lime or lemon zest and juice over. Season well, and trickle the oil over. Cook the salmon under the hot broiler for 2 minutes. Turn the slices, and cook for 2 minutes, until the fish is firm and cooked. Do not overcook or the salmon will be dry. Then place under the broiler for a further 2 minutes, until crisp and golden. Spread half the watercress over the bottom half of the bread. Sprinkle with the capers. Arrange the salmon slices on top, overlapping them slightly. Then spoon the remaining cooking juices over. Sprinkle with the chives and top with the remaining watercress. Replace the top of the loaf and cut to serve.

Alternatively, wrap the loaf tightly in plastic wrap and allow to cool completely. Slice the loaf when cold.

ingredients

1 large ciabatta

9 oz/250 g skinless boneless salmon fillet

grated zest of 1 lime or lemon and juice of $1/2$ lime or lemon

salt and pepper

2 tbsp olive oil

large bag of watercress, tough stalks discarded

1 tbsp capers

2 tbsp snipped fresh chives

Toasted Eggplant & Anchovy
Focaccia with Goat Cheese

serves 4

Preheat the broiler on a medium–high setting. Slice the focaccia in half horizontally and lay on the rack in the broiler pan. Toast the underside of the bread, and cut side of the top half, for about 2 minutes, until browned.

Drain and reserve the oil from the anchovies. Remove the bread and lay the eggplant slices on the rack. Brush with the reserved oil and broil for 4–5 minutes, until well browned.

Chop the anchovies and mix with the scallions. Arrange the eggplant slices and cheese on the bread, covering the untoasted surfaces of the bottom and the top of the loaf (or the tops of both flatbreads). Top with the anchovy mixture. Brush the remaining oil lightly over the eggplant. Broil for 3–4 minutes, until browned.

Purée the basil, cilantro, lemon zest, and olive oil in a blender. Top the bottom half of bread with tomatoes and add the other half on top, eggplant slices up. Cut into wedges. Serve drizzled with the herb oil.

ingredients

1 thick focaccia loaf (about 6–7 inches/15–17 cm) or 2 Italian flatbreads

2 oz/55 g canned anchovies in olive oil

1 eggplant, about 9 oz/250 g, thinly sliced

6 scallions, chopped

5 oz/140 g goat cheese log, thinly sliced

handful of basil leaves

handful of fresh cilantro leaves

grated zest of 1 lemon

4 tbsp olive oil

10–12 cherry tomatoes, halved

Creamy Pan-glazed Pork with Grapes on Walnut Toasts

serves 4–8

Mix the grapes with the lime rind and a squeeze of juice, and set aside. Preheat the broiler on a medium–high setting. Trim the crusts off the bread. Heat together the olive oil and the butter, then remove from the heat. Brush both sides of the bread slices sparingly with some of the butter and oil.

Toast the bread on the rack in the broiler pan for 2 minutes on each side. Cut each toast into four and keep hot in the warm broiler. Meanwhile, add the garlic, bay leaf, and rosemary to the oil in the pan and heat. Add the onion and stir-fry for about 2 minutes, until soft but not browned. Add the pork and fry over fairly high heat for 3–4 minutes, stirring frequently, until lightly browned.

Add the celery with seasoning and stir-fry for 2–3 minutes until the celery is lightly cooked and the pork well browned. Discard the herbs. Place the toasts on the plates. Top with the pork, using a slotted spoon. Keep hot.

Replace the pan on the heat, add the brandy and cook over high heat, scraping all the cooking juices off the pan. Boil hard for about a minute. Add the cream and bring to a boil, stirring. Remove from the heat and stir in the parsley. Drizzle over the pork. Add the grapes and serve.

ingredients

6 oz/170 g seedless green grapes, halved

zest of 1 lime and a squeeze of juice

4 slices walnut bread (about $1/2$ inch/1 cm thick)

2 tbsp olive oil

2 tbsp butter

1 garlic clove, chopped

1 bay leaf

1 rosemary sprig

1 small onion, halved and thinly sliced

12 oz/340 g lean boneless pork, cut into thin strips

2 celery stalks, very thinly sliced

salt and pepper

4 tbsp brandy

$1/2$ cup heavy cream

2 tbsp chopped fresh parsley

Avocado Shrimp Toasts

serves 4–8

Finely chop the shrimp in a food processor. Add the cornstarch, egg white and seasoning, and pulse once or twice to mix to a coarse paste. Do not over-process the mixture or it will become too thin. Transfer to a bowl and mix in the lemon zest, celery, parsley, and chives.

Preheat the broiler on a medium–high setting. Brush the bread lightly with butter on both sides and toast on the rack in the broiler pan for 2 minutes on each side. The pan must not be too near the heat.

Reduce the heat to medium–low. Trim the very edges of the crusts off the toasts and divide the shrimp mixture among them, spreading it out evenly to cover the bread completely. Broil for 1 minute, until the mixture is lightly set, then brush with the remaining butter. Cook for 3–4 minutes, until set and golden.

Halve, pit, peel, and dice the avocados. Whisk the lemon juice with the mustard, tarragon, and seasoning. Gradually whisk in the oil.

Cut the cooked toasts into quarters and place on warmed plates. Top with the avocado, the lemon dressing, and garnish with the tarragon sprigs and serve.

ingredients

2 cups peeled cooked shrimps, thawed if frozen

2 tbsp cornstarch

1 egg white

salt and pepper

grated zest of 1 lemon

1 celery stalk, finely chopped

2 tbsp chopped fresh parsley

4 tbsp snipped fresh chives

4 medium–thick slices good white bread

$1/4$ cup butter, melted

2 avocados

1 tbsp lemon juice

$1/2$ tsp Dijon mustard (or other type, to taste)

1 tbsp tarragon

3 tbsp olive oil

fresh tarragon sprigs, to garnish

Glazed Beets & Egg
Sourdough Toasties

serves 2–4

Boil the eggs for 8 minutes, then drain, peel, and chop them. Set aside. Dice the beets quite small and place in a small bowl. Mix in half the sugar, 1 tsp of the cider vinegar, and seasoning.

Preheat the broiler on a medium–high setting. Brush the bread with a little olive oil and toast on the rack in the broiler pan for 2–3 minutes, until crisp and golden.

Meanwhile, trickle 1 tsp of the remaining oil over the beets. Whisk the remaining cider vinegar, mustard, and remaining sugar together with seasoning. Gradually whisk in the remaining oil to make a thick dressing. Stir in the dill and taste for seasoning—it should be sweet and mustardy, with a sharpness—add more sugar or vinegar if you wish.

Turn the bread and top with the beets, giving it a stir first, covering the slices right up to the crusts. Glaze the beets under the broiler for 2–3 minutes, until browned in places.

Cut the bread slices in half or quarters and top with egg. Drizzle with a little dressing, garnish with the dill sprigs and serve immediately.

ingredients

4 eggs

1 lb 2 oz/500 g cooked beets (fresh or vacuum-packed without vinegar)

2 tsp sugar

5 tsp apple cider vinegar

salt and pepper

4 slices sourdough bread (from a long oval loaf)

6 tbsp olive oil

1 tbsp Dijon mustard

3 tbsp chopped fresh dill

dill sprigs, to garnish

Italian
Steak Heroes

serves 4

Preheat the broiler on a medium–high setting. Heat the olive oil in a large pan over medium heat. Add the onion, garlic, bell pepper, and mushrooms, and cook, stirring occasionally, for 5–10 minutes until softened and beginning to brown.

Add the ground steak and cook, stirring frequently and breaking up any lumps with a wooden spoon, for 5 minutes, or until browned on all sides. Add the wine, tomato paste, and salt and pepper to taste and let simmer for 10 minutes, stirring occasionally. Remove from the heat.

Split the ciabatta rolls in half and brush both halves with extra virgin olive oil. Toast lightly under the preheated broiler. Put the bottom halves onto a piece of foil and spoon an equal quantity of the sauce on top of each.

Slice the cheese, then divide among the roll bottoms and arrange on top of the sauce. Add the basil leaves and cover with the tops of the rolls. Press down gently and grill under a low heat, for 5–10 minutes or until golden. Leave the sandwiches for at least 1 hour before serving.

ingredients

1 tbsp olive oil

1 small onion, finely chopped

1 garlic clove, finely chopped

1 small red bell pepper, cored, seeded, and finely chopped

$3^1/_2$ oz/100 g white mushrooms, finely chopped

$^7/_8$ cup freshly ground steak

$^1/_2$ cup red wine

2 tbsp tomato paste

salt and pepper

4 ciabatta rolls

extra virgin olive oil, for brushing

$2^3/_4$ oz/75 g mozzarella cheese

2 tbsp torn fresh basil leaves

Pear & Roquefort
Open-face Sandwiches

serves 2–4

Preheat the broiler on a medium–high setting. Put the bread slices under the broiler and toast until crisp, but not brown, on both sides. Do not turn off the broiler.

Fold or cut the ham slices to cover each slice of bread, then divide the pear slices equally between the breads. Lay the cheese slices on top.

Return the breads to the broiler until the cheese melts and bubbles. Serve.

ingredients

4 slices walnut bread or pain Poilâne, about $1/2$ inch/1 cm thick

4 thin slices cured ham, such as Bayonne or prosciutto

2 ripe dessert pears, such as Conference, peeled, halved, cored, and thinly sliced lengthwise

$3^{1}/_{2}$ oz/100 g Roquefort cheese, very thinly sliced

Focaccia with Roasted Cherry Tomatoes, Basil & Crispy Pancetta

serves 4–6

Place the flour, dried basil, sugar, yeast, and salt in a bowl. Combine the water and oil and mix with the dry ingredients to form a soft dough, adding more water if the dough appears too dry. Turn out onto a lightly floured counter and knead for 10 minutes, or until the dough bounces back when pressed lightly with your finger. Place the dough in a lightly oiled bowl and cover with plastic wrap. Leave in a warm place for 1 hour, or until doubled in size.

Meanwhile, preheat the oven to 275°F/140°C. Place the tomatoes on a baking sheet covered with parchment paper, sprinkle with oil, and season to taste with salt and pepper. Bake for 30 minutes, or until the tomatoes are soft. Increase the oven temperature to 425°F/220°C. Remove the dough from the bowl and knead again briefly. Shape into a rectangle and place on a lightly oiled baking sheet, turning the dough over to oil both sides. Make rough indentations in the dough using your fingers. Top with the tomatoes and pancetta. Sprinkle with salt and pepper. Leave in a warm place for 10 minutes for the dough to rise again. Bake for 15–20 minutes, or until golden brown and cooked through. Drizzle with oil and top with fresh basil. Serve warm.

ingredients

1 lb 2 oz/500 g white bread flour, plus extra for kneading and rolling

1 tbsp dried basil

$1/2$ tsp sugar

2 tsp active dry yeast

2 tsp salt

$1^1/4$ cups lukewarm water

2 tbsp olive oil, plus extra for oiling

topping

14 oz/400 g cherry tomatoes

1 tbsp olive oil, plus extra for oiling and drizzling

salt and pepper

7 oz/200 g thick pancetta, diced

4 tbsp chopped fresh basil

Double Chocolate
Mango Brioche

serves 4

Preheat the broiler on a medium–high setting and toast the brioche slices on both sides, well away from the heat, until crisp and browned. Remove, and leave to cool for a couple of minutes on a rack.

Increase the heat to the hottest setting and lay a piece of cooking foil on the rack in the broiler pan. Trim off and discard the edges of the crusts from the toasts. Spread the toasts generously with chocolate spread, as thick as you prefer, taking it right up to the edges.

Place the toasts on the foil. Arrange the mango slices on top, and sprinkle the sugar over them. Sprinkle with the lime zest and juice. Broil for 1–2 minutes—just long enough to melt the sugar, and make the fruit, and its dressing, hot on the surface.

Top with chocolate ice cream and crème fraîche. Decorate with lime slices, if liked, and serve immediately.

ingredients

4 thick slices brioche loaf (about 1–1$\frac{1}{2}$ inches/3.5 cm thick)

3–4 tbsp good-quality chocolate spread

1 large mango, peeled, pitted, and thinly sliced

4 tsp sugar

grated zest and juice of 1 lime

4 scoops good-quality dark chocolate ice cream

4 tbsp crème fraîche or Greek-style yogurt

lime slices, to decorate (optional)

Spiced French Toast
with Seasonal Berries

serves 4

Preheat the oven to 425°F/220°C. Put the eggs and egg white in a large, shallow bowl or dish and whisk together with a fork. Add the cinnamon and allspice and whisk until combined.

To prepare the berry topping, put the sugar and orange juice in a pan and bring to a boil over low heat, stirring until the sugar has dissolved. Add the berries, then remove from the heat and let cool for 10 minutes.

Meanwhile, soak the bread slices in the egg mixture for about 1 minute on each side. Brush a large baking sheet with the melted butter and place the bread slices on the sheet. Bake in the preheated oven for 5–7 minutes, or until lightly browned. Turn the slices over and bake for an additional 2–3 minutes. Serve the berries spooned over the toast and decorate with the mint sprigs.

ingredients

4 eggs, plus 1 extra egg white

$1/4$ tsp ground cinnamon

$1/4$ tsp allspice

4 slices thick white bread

1 tbsp unsalted butter, melted

fresh mint sprigs, to decorate

berry topping

scant $1/2$ cup superfine sugar

$1/4$ cup freshly squeezed orange juice

$10^1/2$ oz/300 g mixed fresh seasonal berries, such as strawberries, raspberries, and blueberries, picked over and hulled